# No Parenthesis: A Reflection of Loss

## Allyson Valfre

Presentation by *BookLeaf Publishing*

Web: www.bookleafpub.com

E-mail: info@bookleafpub.com

ISBN: 9789358317626

First edition 2024

*Mom ~ you were my first critic and my biggest fan. I hope these words make it to you.*

# ACKNOWLEDGEMENT

To my best friends who always push me to be a better writer and a better person. Thank you for accepting me in all my forms.

# Loyalty I

When my mom got sick, I hadn't spoken to her
in nearly four years. The call came out of the
blue

her name appearing on my screen; a rock the
size of a bowling ball dropped into my

stomach.

I remember her being angry. Angry that she was
having to call me

(of all people)

to tell me she's going to die. She was scared too

but I clearly remember feeling bad that I upset
her. That I

intruded

on her fear and forced her to make a call she
clearly didn't want to.

Even so, I dropped everything. I drove the seven
hours

down I-5 to prove that I was still her daughter,

still a person she could
                      trust.

She wasn't doing well then but she played it off,
our nerves at seeing each other again

Taut like a high wire tightrope act.

She ended up in the hospital not too long after
that. She told me not to worry,

the doctors were just being overly

cautious.

I wished I could believe her.
My emotions warring inside me.

Were we just supposed to pretend nothing
happened in those four years?

I got the call from an ER doctor while I was at
work.

"You need to get down here.
I don't think she has much longer.
I would say three weeks top."

# Family Tradition

Grandmother was a weaver                    of
fabric.
She collected               scraps of cloth and
               Transformed them,
Like magic,
                    Into her legacy.


Grandfather was                    an adventurer.
He        hiked,        climbed,        skied,
and
          Traveled the                    world,
Bringing it home        with him
And making it                    his legacy.


Mama was a                    painter.
She saw the world                    through the
          Tip of her               pencil and
Brought it to life        through brushstrokes,
Framing just a        piece of her legacy.

Brother was a musician.
          He beat out               rhythm
with a

Trumpet                 and his soul,
          Making the notes
dance
Playing            his legacy.


And what am I?
          A weaver                not of thread,
but of words
An explorer      of the page                    chapter
by chapter
I                    draw breath into          words,
          paragraphs,      poems,
I        play with letters        likes music
notes.

# Grandfather's House

Grandfather's house is nestled in the hills
with its crisp, blue sky
And the oak trees that remind me of him.
Inside, there is a little garden
Which contains all of the love
Grandfather radiated into this little house.

My childhood is imprinted in that house,
Tucked up in the hills
Where it bloomed flowers and love
Alike under the cool California sky.
There is a tiny swing nestled in the garden
One made for me just from him.

The wooden swing was made by him
When I was born, preparing the little house
With its beautiful little garden
For the first grandchild that would roam its hills,
And bloom under the grand sky
Nurtured with laughter and love.

It was here that I first learned love,
A love given so freely by him
As he held my hand under the big sky
While we paraded around the little house

And explored the surrounding hills
Before returning to the little garden.

There is a tiny sandbox in the little garden,
That he made with all his love
For his grandchild who would roam the hills
But would always come back to him
And the beloved little house
Under the clear blue sky.

Even today, when I stand under that same sky,
Or when I walk through the garden,
Or just stand in that house,
I am reminded of all his love
And everything that defined him
When he lived in those hills.

And for me, those hills will always reflect the
wide open sky,
And everything that was made by him in that
little garden
Will always remind me of the love he so freely
gave in that little house.

# Tache

I look at photographs
and see nothing of my grandmother
in me.
My long dark hair
stands opposite of her short,
light locks.
Our noses differ in two different
directions
and my eyes are
the eyes of another woman.
But I carry her spirit with me.

Some days, Mama would look at me
and say, "You are just like your grandmother!"
in a funny voice.
When I twirl my hair
absentmindedly
I am just like my aunt;
When I drove her crazy,
I became my father.
But in the quiet moments,
moments that I don't even
recognize as particular,
I am my strong grand-mère.

We share the same tache,
the same mark on our hearts.
and when I place my hand on
the art she left behind, her quilt
upon my shoulders, it reminds me
of the person she was,
a person I still hope
to become.

# Photographs

Why do you always
look so sad
In every photograph
A permanent tiny frown

I search desperately for a
Genuine smile
One that reaches past
Your cheekbones

Were you happy in that
blue green dress?
Your hand protectively
on your stomach

Knowing that I was
Waiting
within you
Or did you worry?

Unsure of what the world
May inflict on you,
Your child,
Your heart?

There is a shift
In the photos
I sift through
Where did you go?

No longer in the frame
Did your smile ever meet
Your eyes
While you stood behind it?

Did you laugh
As I flew down the hill?
In my pink puffer
The sled beneath me

Did you smile
Looking through the
Camera lens
As I held my little brother?

I pray that you did
That the same smile
That graces my lips
Met yours

I hope that you were
Happy like I was
That you remembered
The little joys

I'll fill in your smile
With my own
As I take in the memories
That you left behind

# Loyalty II

I stayed three weeks, watching the steady up

down of her lungs straining for air.

Waiting for them to stop.

When the fourth week slipped by, I started to get
worried about work and

my life outside of the hospital room.

I had told my employer that I would be gone for
at least a month but…

she wasn't dead.

In fact, one day she sat up and said

"I'm hungry."

In a momentous turn of events, my
cancer-ridden mother took a turn
for the better.

She continued to feel better for four more years.

During those years, we never discussed what
had happened between us.

Sometimes we half-heartedly talked about the
past

or casually danced around the idea of

before.

But we never confronted what happened.

I never heard her say, "I'm sorry."

I never asked her to say *I'm sorry*.

# The love you give

I model your affection like a fur coat
Ribbons of love shiny on my skin
The stern lines of this adoration corset
Taut and needy
If I hold my breath just like this
Will you capture the moment?
The spark of pride
That I foster within my rib cage
My bones the flint
My lungs the bellows
Woosh
Can I stoke the flames?

# January

January is the coldest month
I never knew how cold it was
Without you

The morning you left
A feeling I couldn't name
Relief? Guilt? Fear?

I kept it bottled nice and warm
Right in the center of my chest
Until it burned its way

Up & out of my throat
A sound I didn't know
I was capable of making

As I lay on the shower floor
The water warm against my skin
But all I could feel was

Cold
Deep
Down

My heart

a stone
in my chest.

# Stains

today i found a stain
i don't know where it came from
how do i get it out?

i've scrubbed til my fingers are raw
used all the soap i could find
soaked it in cold

what do you do with a stain
that persists?
a stain with life and tenacity?

how do you remove
what doesn't want to leave?
that which wants to be remembered?

or should the question be
how do you live with a stain
that you earned?

a stain you created
a constant reminder of the things
you'd rather forget?

that's the thing about stains

they leave an imprint that
sometimes you just can't get out

# Dream Walking

I believe in the power of dreams
Can they act as a portal
Between my world and yours?

Can you breach the void
And meet me here?
For even a moment

I just want to hear your voice
But as you walk in my dreams
You feel just out of reach

A version of you that I don't know
Your face small and sad
As if there's something you can't say

Or won't tell me.
What words can span
that great distance?

I am not content
To wait for you
My eyes open and

I awake alone

Your face fading
In the aftermath

# New Normal

My new normal includes
Avoiding looking at your name in my phone
& pretending like I'm okay with that

This new normal also means
No more driving home phone calls
Or weekend updates or messages of any kind

Now normal means that when I drive by
Your street I keep my head facing forward
& resist the urge to put my blinker on

Normal is feeling less panic daily
But emptiness in greater magnitude
A hole so deep that sometimes I feel like

Tossing myself into it
Just to see if there's another side
Or an end somewhere that I can't see

I'm starting to learn that
There is no end, no "other side"
To grief

So new normal is pretending that the hole

Doesn't exist, isn't growing, isn't empty
Isn't there at all

The thing is…
The new normal
Isn't normal at all

# Loyalty III

I stayed out of misguided loyalty.

I made sure that she knew I was
there

in hopes that it would bring me peace

for the years I missed.

I stayed to earn back the title of
                "daughter."

I spent four years driving up and down

every weekend

just to prove that I was a good person.

That I didn't abandon her.

Not the way she had me.

I don't regret my choices.

I have a thousand new happy memories

from the four years that we reconciled.

I hope that she knew that I loved her

and forgave her without saying it.

She forgave me without saying it.

But when I think of the immense pressure

I put on myself to be loyal

That little girl inside still doesn't know if she made
                        a difference.

 If she spent enough time
          and money


and effort.

# A Single Year

It was October when you told me that you were
done                    fighting
The weather was still warm,
we had just finished eating
The Chinese food still heavy in my
stomach
I told you that I understood because
                    I did
You had held on for so long, I could see you
were                         tired
November came                         and
went, your appetite fluctuating
But you ate all of our thanksgiving dinner
And asked for seconds, which made my wife
beam                    from head to toe
She wasn't my wife then but you knew
she would be
And I think that made you
sad
Because you knew
        you wouldn't be there
But you loved her so much,              you
made sure to be excited
Christmas was a                    blur

Food     and movies      and making sure
you didn't exert yourself
But I was tired too;                    I didn't
appreciate the moment
When January dawned                     I didn't
know what to expect
Your sister came down and it felt like a
                        verdict
Even though you were still as sharp
and strong            as usual
You passed away                   only 28
days into the year
And to this day
I still wasn't ready
I married her in February
I think you would have      liked the
ceremony
I should have married her            sooner
to be honest,          so you could be there
A selfish moment                  on two
parts
We put you              to rest in April
And the woods were cool
and calm            and perfect
I hope you are happy                there
It's October again, my birthday come
and gone
The first one                       without
you

And I can't help          but think how much
good      has come from this year
Good that you didn't get to                    see
It hurts being happy
                    without you.
But I think               you would be proud
That my           life      is still                moving
forward
That I carry               your voice with me
I miss you
Mama.

# Death is no parenthesis

I hope this is true
No period to mark the page
But an ellipsis
A page break with
a detailed illustration of
the journey taken
The next chapter
Simply a turn of the page
A settling of ink
The words waiting to be read
To be brought to life
for life's not a paragraph
and death (I hope) is no parenthesis

"[since feeling is first]"; e.e. cummings, 1926

# Why green has become my new favorite color

You surrounded your home
With green

Rosemary sprigs
Cilantro leaves

Chile peppers in summer
Flowering trees in spring

Avocado tree bearing fruit
Heavy and ripe

Green tea in a tiny pot
Ceramic swirls of sea green

Aloe vera stalks
For clumsy daughters

Limes for margaritas
And frogs for rainy weather

A green thumb that you
Didn't pass down

Hazel eyes sprinkled
With green

Emerald necklaces
Citrine earrings

It's the color that feels
Most like home

That feels most
Like you

# paint by numbers

my body is art
each scar and dark spot
a different color
paint me by numbers

my lovers each lay down
a new color
fill in a new section
paint me by numbers

i'm not fond of the colors
she left behind
they've faded to grays
paint me by numbers

his colors have been painted over
but they were all beiges and off-whites
it's easy to miss them
paint me by numbers

your colors are vibrant
purples, pinks, yellows, teal
they fill up the most space

and bring me joy on each viewing
a constant reminder that i am yours
and you've painted me whole

# Let's Stay Home

"We should get ready…"
You say with as much enthusiasm
as someone
Preparing for a  double            root canal
And I sigh with                matching
energy
Because that's
absolutely
what we          should do
But currently your head is on            my
shoulder
And the warmth of your                body
        next to mine
Is too          delicious to move away from
The arm you've thrown across    my belly
Delightfully      heavy            and
comforting
Our legs          entwined in a    complicated
puzzle
That just feels too        challenging to extract
        myself from
Your breath      skitters down my chest
Your lungs        rising and falling
in a pattern
That matches my own

And I fear that   I'll never find a position
As comfortable as the one                    we've
fallen into
From now on              any movement
away from you
Will be an               excruciating     torment
of the
Machiavellian            kind
And that's just          too much to risk
"Or… we could just stay home?"
The words barely                     out of my
mouth
Before I feel you        nestle your way
Closer than                          physically
possible
A breach of              physics           and
space
More pleasing than any other
scientific discovery
In the history of mankind

"Yeah, let's stay home"

# Horse Girl

All I ever wanted
As a little girl
Was to have my own horse
That would carry me far away

That would love me
From the first stroke
Of my hand on its forelock
And risk it all to protect me

A dancing stallion
Rearing up on hind legs
Black as the midnight sky
Its muzzle a stark white

Or a sweet bay mare
Her brown eyes
Reflections of mine
Docile & motherly

I dared not beg for one
I knew the cost
& feared upsetting
My single mother

But I dreamed
every day of
leaving my life
on horseback

My mother did what
She could & bought
Books & games
& movies about horses

I absorbed them all
Hungrily, never sated
Dreaming of the day
When one could be mine

I grew up too fast
& left my horse fantasies
Behind me, no more time
For childish play

I was embarrassed of my
Fanaticism, my fervor
A childish, silly game
Long meant to be left behind

But when I cleared out
Her home, I found the boxes
The books, the figurines
Of my childhood love

She kept them all
A reminder of the child me
The little girl
who could dream

# Loyalty IV

Now that she's gone,                     there is
a new sense of loyalty,
a sense of loyalty to her memory.
I remember when my parents
divorced
how fiercely loyal I was
to my mother.
I didn't want to say          or think of
                anything
that could remotely                   betray her.
I grew up wanting to     protect her
in ways that no child
could accomplish.
I wanted to protect her
in the ways                          I
                should have been protected.
I fear this
blind loyalty                of her memory.
I fear forgetting                   the bad things,
the things that shouldn't have happened
                but did.
Because death is no free pass,
it doesn't erase   what was done  or said in the
past.
It doesn't wipe  your slate clean.

But I don't want to lose myself
to the anger                    or the hurt.
I have held on to anger
for far too long.
                    I want to let it go.

                              I have

to let her go.

# Reminiscence

To the color green
in all its shades
To stormy sunny days
To mystery books
& detective shows
To art & music &
Fabric, thread & cloth
To handmade jewelry
& ceramic bowls
To wine & French cheese
To champagne
To the things that remind me
Of you & make me smile
& the things that
Make me cry
To dry eyes but
Heavy hearts
To unbearable sharp feelings
To laughter & to pain
To you in every form
Here & away
Pour vous
À bientôt